Rocks and Minerals

By Kris Hirschmann

World Discovery Science Readers™

SCHOLASTIC INC.

New York • Toronto • London • Auckland • Sydney
Mexico City • New Delhi • Hong Kong • Buenos Aires

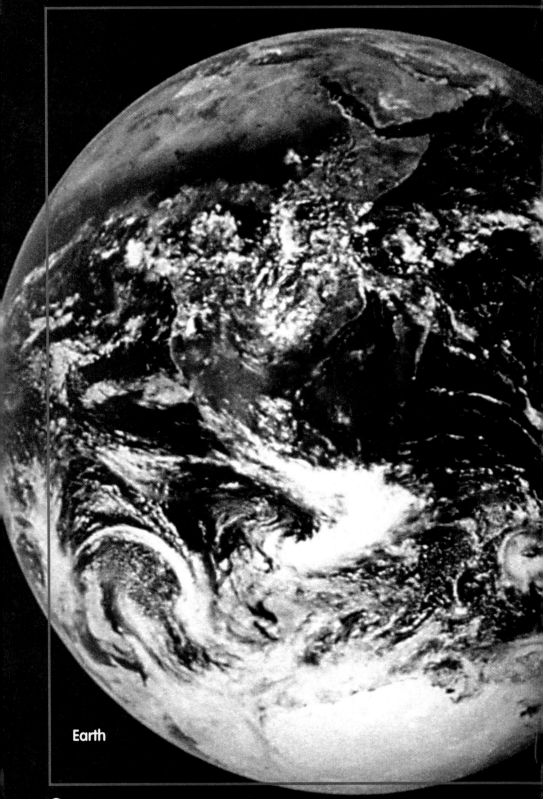

Earth

Chapter 1

What Are Minerals?

Our solar sytem was once a giant cloud of dust. The dust pieces were made of hard, nonliving materials called **minerals**. Over time, the minerals began to stick together to form Earth and all the other planets.

There are about 3,500 known types of minerals. A mineral is made of specific **elements** arranged in certain ways. The elements and the arrangement are always the same. This means that each mineral has features that never change.

Earth's hard outer layer, also called its **crust** is made mostly of eight elements. This chart shows the most common elements.

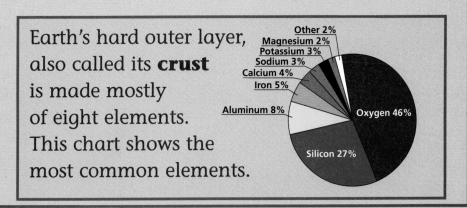

Other 2%
Magnesium 2%
Potassium 3%
Sodium 3%
Calcium 4%
Iron 5%
Aluminum 8%
Oxygen 46%
Silicon 27%

People can identify minerals by looking for certain features. A mineral's color is the first clue to its identity. Malachite, for example, is always green, and sulfur is always yellow. Minerals may also be black, white, red, or almost any other color you can imagine.

Streak is another clue. Streak is the color a mineral leaves when you rub it against a white tile. Different minerals leave different streaks. Realgar, for example, leaves an orange-red streak. Pyrite leaves a greenish-black streak.

Malachite

Sulfur

Realgar

Hardness is also important. Some minerals, like talc are so soft that you can scratch it with your fingernail. Other minerals, like diamonds, are so hard that they cannot be scratched by a steel file.

Mineral hardness is ranked on a scale of 1 to 10. This scale is called the Mohs' Scale. The softest is 1 and the hardest is 10. Minerals with higher numbers can scratch those with lower numbers.

1	Talc	6	Orthoclase
2	Gypsum	7	Quartz
3	Calcite	8	Topaz
4	Fluorite	9	Corundum
5	Apatite	10	Diamond

Pyrite

Minerals can also be identified by their **crystal structure.**

Some crystals, like pyrite and garnet, are perfectly square in structure. Other crystals are long and thin with pointy tips. Some crystals look rectangular, and some may even be hexagonal, which means it has six equal sides.

All crystals have something called **habit**. Habit is the way groups of crystals grow together. The crystals of some minerals, like hematite, grow in round clumps. Scientists say hematite has a **globular** habit.

Hematite

Australian Selenite

Mexican Rose Selenite

Malachite with Calcite

Other crystals also grow as bunches of needles, piles of cubes, or rocky sheets stuck together. Habit can make crystals very easy to identify.

Table salt is a square crystal. Look at some grains of salt with a magnifying glass to see their shape.

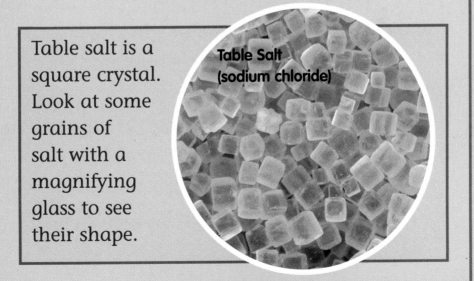

Table Salt (sodium chloride)

Quartz

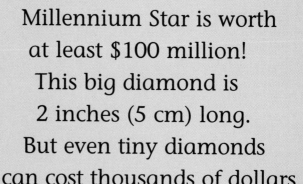

Calcite

Some crystals are very common, and others are very rare. Quartz and calcite are two crystals that can be found just about everywhere.

Diamonds, emeralds, and some other crystals are hard to find. Rare crystals are called **gemstones**.

Gemstones can be very valuable. One diamond called the Millennium Star is worth at least $100 million! This big diamond is 2 inches (5 cm) long. But even tiny diamonds can cost thousands of dollars.

Diamond

Gemstones come in many different colors. The best diamonds are perfectly clear, with no color at all. Sapphires are blue, and rubies are a rich red. Gemstones may also be green, yellow, orange, and many other pretty colors.

Uncut Rubies, Jade, Sapphires

Silver

Gold in Quartz

Gold, silver, and some other **metallic** minerals are rare and valuable. These minerals are called precious metals.

Erupting Volcano

Chapter 2

How Rocks Form

Rocks are made of minerals mixed together. A rock may contain just a couple of minerals, or it may contain many different types.

There are three rock families: **igneous**, **sedimentary**, and **metamorphic**. All rocks fall into one of these families. A rock's family name tells us something about how the rock was formed.

It is easy to see the different mineral chips in this piece of granite. Granite is made up of the minerals quartz, feldspar, and mica.

Granite

Cooled Lava

Igneous rocks form when a hot liquid deep within the earth, called **magma**, cools and gets hard. Magma sometimes moves toward the surface through cracks in the crust. The magma hardens into rock if it reaches a place where the temperature is cool enough.

Igneous rocks that form inside the crust are called **intrusive** igneous rocks. Pegmatite and other types of granite are common intrusive rocks.

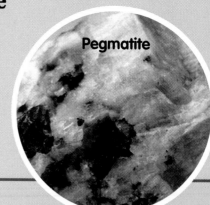

Pegmatite

Obsidian and pumice form when volcanoes erupt. Obsidian is jet-black and smooth like glass. Pumice is gray and full of holes. It floats in water!

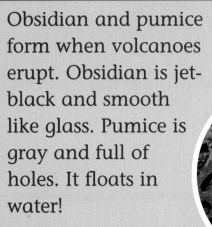

Obsidian

Pumice

Sometimes magma reaches the earth's surface through volcanoes or other holes. Then it is called **lava**. Lava cools very quickly after it comes in contact with water or air. It hardens into rocks. Rocks formed in this way are called **extrusive** igneous rocks. Basalt is the most common extrusive rock.

Basalt

Sedimentary rocks form when many small particles stick together. The particles might be rock or mineral chips. They could also be little bits of plants or animals. Particles can be very fine, as in sandstone. They can also be big, as in **conglomerates**.

Sandstone

Limestone is made of the stuck-together shells and bones of dead sea creatures. These shells and bones fell to the ocean floor over millions of years. Eventually, pressure pushed them together and they became rocks. You can see the shells in some limestone rocks if you look closely.

Limestone

Shell

Clay

Sedimentary rocks are softer than other kinds of rocks. Some are so soft that you can break them with your bare hands! Clay and chalk are two easy-to-break sedimentary rocks.

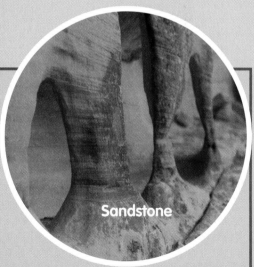

Deserts contain lots of sandstone. Wind sometimes **erodes** this sedimentary rock into amazing shapes.

Sandstone

Metamorphic rocks were once igneous or sedimentary rocks. But heat and pressure changed them into something different.

Most metamorphic rocks form in places where mountains are being made. Mountains are created when parts of Earth's crust bump into one another. The bumping causes lots of heat and pressure. This heat and pressure changes the structure of rocks. Limestone, for example, turns into marble.

Gneiss

Slate

A sedimentary rock called shale turns into slate, schist, or gneiss, depending on the amount of pressure.

Rocks can also be changed by heat alone. This happens when a rock is close to magma or lava. The rock turns into something new if it gets hot enough.

Large grain

Small grain

Metamorphic rocks that form at low temperatures and pressures have small grains. Those rocks that form at high temperatures and pressures have large grains.

Sandstone and dried clay in
the American Southwest

Chapter 3

Keys to the Past

Rocks last a long time. Many of the rocks we see on our planet's surface are hundreds of millions of years old. A few are even older. One rocky area in Canada is thought to be about 3.9 billion years old!

Old rocks hold clues to Earth's past. Scientists called **geologists** study rocks to learn about things that happened long, long ago.

Over time, different types of rocks pile up in layers. The bottom layers are the oldest, and the top layers are the youngest.

Peak of Mount Everest

Rocks show us that Earth did not always look the way it does today. All of the planet's landmasses were once jammed together. They slowly drifted apart to form our modern-day continents. Scientists know this because they have found the exact same rocks on different continents.

This picture shows which parts of the United States and Canada were once underwater.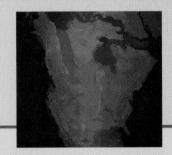

Rocks also prove that some dry areas were once oceans. The midwestern United States, for example, was covered with water 65 million years ago. How do we know this? The area contains rocks that form only in the sea.

Even the world's tallest mountain was once underwater. Mount Everest has sea rocks near its peak.

Mount Everest from afar

Some rocks show signs of plants and animals that lived a long time ago. These types of rocks are called **fossils**.

Dinosaur fossil

Most fossils formed when dead plants or animals fell into mud or another gooey substance. The soft parts of the plants or animals rotted away, but the harder parts did not. They stayed in the mud. Eventually, the mud turned into sedimentary rock. The plant and animal remains were trapped inside.

Fish fossil

Trace fossils

Sedimentary
rocks may also
contain fossil footprints,
leaf prints, and other signs of ancient life.
These are called trace fossils.

Fossils are not usually found in
igneous or metamorphic rocks. The heat
that creates these rocks ruins fossils.

Trilobites are common
fossils. These sea
creatures
became
extinct
about 250
million years ago.

Trilobite

Grand Canyon

Rock **formations** also tell us about the past. They teach us about the forces that shape Earth's surface.

The Grand Canyon is one of our planet's most amazing rock formations. It is 217 miles (349 km) long, 4 to 18 miles (6 to 29 km) wide, and

Dripping water creates cave rocks. How? Each drop leaves a little bit of sediment behind when it falls. Rocks created in this way are called stalactites.

Stalactites

more than 1 mile (1.6 km) deep. The Colorado River carved the Grand Canyon out of solid rock. It did this by carrying away tiny rock bits over millions of years.

Volcanic plugs also provide clues to the past. These rock formations were once magma inside volcanoes. The magma cooled into rock. Then wind, rain, and other forces removed the outer layer of the volcano. Only the plug remained.

Devil's Tower, Montana

North American Petroglyphs (rock paintings)

Chapter 3
People and Rocks

Rocks and minerals have many uses. The earliest people used powdered rocks to make colorful paints. They used chipped flint and other hard minerals to make arrowheads. They also pounded rocks together to grind food.

Today, people use rocks and minerals for thousands of things. These substances are in our houses, our computers, our wristwatches, and our TVs. They are also in roads, jewelry, fireplaces, and food. Life would not be the same without rocks!

Azurite

Hematite

Powdered hematite makes red paint. Powdered azurite makes blue paint.

The construction, electronics, and jewelry industries depend on rocks and minerals. Builders use soft minerals like gypsum to make the inside walls of houses. They use hard rocks like marble to build floors. Sand and pebbles are mixed with other substances to make concrete and bricks.

Sand

Marble

Minerals are used in the electronics industry. For example, tiny quartz crystals help watches to keep time. Silicon and sapphire chips help computers to run. Copper is used to make wires.

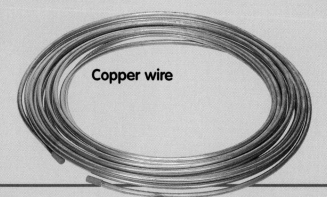

Copper wire

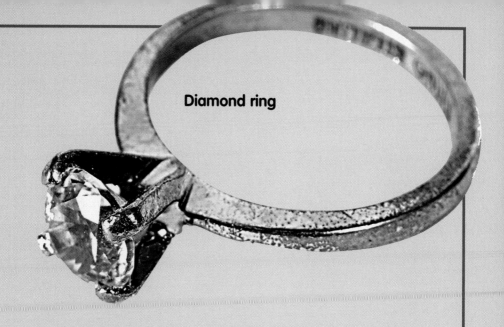

Diamond ring

The jewelry industry also depends on rocks and minerals. Mineral gemstones and pretty rocks are used in necklaces, earrings, rings, and more. Gold, silver, platinum, and other minerals make chains and charms.

Light beams bounce off the inside of a cut gemstone. This makes the gemstone look sparkly.

Rocks and minerals are so common in our everyday lives that many people decide to learn more about them. Some people even collect rocks and minerals as a hobby.

You can start your own rock and mineral collection. Bring home any interesting **specimens** you find. Rinse them well to remove dirt. Then try to identify each one. Use a field guide that lists the features of different rocks and minerals.

First identify your rock and mineral specimens and then label them. Put them where you can see them every day. Why? To remind you of how unique and special each specimen is. Each rock or mineral is a little chunk of Earth's history. By showing your collection, you are putting this history on display every day!

Rock and mineral collections should be labeled and neatly organized.

Glossary

Conglomerates—
[kuhn-GLAHM-muh-ruhts]
Sedimentary rocks with
large particles.

Crust—Earth's hard outer
layer.

Crystal structure—The
shape a mineral takes as it
grows.

Elements—The basic
building blocks of Earth.
There are 106 elements.

Erode—To wear away.

Extrusive—Forming in the
air or water.

Formations—Rocks that
have been shaped by
natural forces such as
wind or rain.

Fossils—Traces of plants and
animals that lived long
ago.

Gemstones—Rare crystals.

Geologists—
[jee-AHL-luh-jihsts]
Scientists who study
Earth's history through
rocks and minerals.

Globular—
[GLAH-byuh-ler] Growing
in round clumps.

Habit—The way groups of
crystals grow together.

Igneous—
[IG-nee-uhs] Formed from
lava or magma.

Intrusive—Forming
underground.

Lava—Liquid rock that
reaches Earth's surface.

Magma—Liquid rock under
Earth's surface.

Metallic—Made of metal.

Metamorphic—
[meh-tuh-MOR-fihk]
Changed by heat,
pressure, or both.

Minerals—Hard, nonliving
substances with a regular
structure.

Sedimentary—
[seh-duh-MEHN-tuh-ree]
Formed when small
particles stick together.

Specimens—Samples.

Streak—The color a mineral
leaves when you rub it
against a white tile.

Volcanic plugs—Rock
formations that were once
magma inside volcanoes.